Building Family Prayer & Traditions

A Redemptorist Publication

Published by
Redemptorist Publications
Alphonsus House Chawton Alton Hampshire GU34 3HQ

Copyright © The Congregation of the Most Holy Redeemer. A Registered Charity

Written by: Steve Givens
Design by: Liz Davies, Roger Smith
Illustrations by: Liz Davies
Photographs: The Image Bank

First Printed   September 1996

ISBN 0 85231 162 1

Printed by: Bourne Press Ltd, Bournemouth, Dorset.

CONTENTS

Introduction

Once family devotions were general, now they are rare. There are reasons for the change. One reason is that the simplicity of the old family life is gone. It is not easy to get all the members of the family together at one time in the day. A part of this is due to less leisure now than formerly ... Indeed the more rapid pace of these modern times magnifies the need for a pause in the day for prayer, some upward look, when for a moment the soul may find an open way between itself and God.

Good words for these fast-paced modern times, right? Well, consider then the fact that the above comes from a devotional book written by *Florence Hobert Perin* in the year 1910. What would she say today I wonder? I think she would say the same thing – we're busy, yet many of us still yearn for that **"moment."** We also yearn to give that moment to our children and instil in them a hunger for God and faith. But how?

It is out of that yearning and confusion that I decided to write this book.

I strongly believe that in prayer and faith lie the answers to many of the problems in our society today. You may disagree, of course, and believe that prayer and "having faith" is a much too simplistic approach to the vast number of complex problems alive in our world today. You may be right, but I won't apologise for my stance. And while I don't believe that we are only called to pray and not put our faith in action to bring about change, I do believe that our lives – grounded in prayer and faith – can affect the world. So, in part, I write this book in response to that age-old question:

"What's wrong with the world?"

We read the newspapers and listen to the radio. We shake our heads and wonder what's gone wrong. Why do people rape, abuse, attack, cheat and kill each other? What drives someone to attack and murder someone he or she doesn't even know? Why do fourteen-year-olds kill each other? I truly believe that the answer lies – at least in part – in the fact that they have no faith in anything outside themselves. They have learned not to trust anyone, much less something like an invisible God. Here's a true story:

A number of years ago I worked as a volunteer in a medium security women's prison. I was part of a rota that offered ecumenical worship services for the women.

One early Saturday morning I walked into the make-shift chapel and saw someone I recognised. It would have been difficult not to have recognised her since her face and her terrifying story had been front-page news for weeks.

Everyone in town knew the story: She had calmly called 911 (the U.S. equivalent of 999) and slowly and methodically explained that she had shot her three young daughters. Later, a television news programme obtained the 911 tape and broadcast it, complete with the truly blood-curdling screams of her children in the background.

All three children had died, and now she sat in the chapel with me.

I began the service, and we sang and prayed and shared thoughts about the theme of the readings for the day: loss of faith. She remained silent and bowed throughout it all. But the word of God and my and the other women's thoughts on faith or the lack of it must have burrowed deep beneath the skin of this woman.

*We paused for a moment of quiet reflection. It was then I saw her head come up. I knew she wanted to say something so I nodded and waited. Finally she spoke: "I think that's what happened to me. **I just lost my faith."***

You could have knocked me and everyone else in the room over with a feather. Her atrocious acts can never be justified and the three young, promising lives can never be brought back. But I don't believe I have ever heard a more poignant argument for the power

and importance of faith in our lives than in those two lines she uttered. More than any homily I have ever heard or any book I've ever read, that woman changed my life. Despite her crime, I am eternally grateful.

This is a rather shocking example of the power of faith, I admit. But it's the first reason I wanted to write this book. Perhaps if her faith had been a bit stronger – perhaps if a parent had sat and prayed with her or gathered her into loving arms and prayed for her – she might have found the strength to go on and let her children live. I believe that anything we do to increase our own faith and build a firmer foundation of faith in our children is worthwhile and will pay long-term benefits for us, them and the world. ***"World peace begins at home"*** is a bumper sticker with which I can heartily agree.

But there's another reason I wanted to write this book. Time for some self-revealing honesty: I'm not an expert about praying with children or building traditions that foster faith. My wife and I have been haphazard at best in our attempts to bring prayer into our home life. But after some soul-searching I decided that one reason – perhaps the chief reason – that we don't pray together as a family as often as we should is that we haven't established any real traditions or rituals for doing so.

I was inspired, in part, to write this book because of a wonderful little book I read by Gabe Huck titled *"How Can I Keep From Singing: Thoughts About Liturgy for Musicians."* What struck me most in Huck's book was his description of ritual and its importance in our lives.

He writes:

> *"[liturgy] can only be what the Church knows how to do, has it in its heart and mind and muscles to do. Liturgy can only be what the Church knows by heart."*

Huck was talking about the liturgy and our participation in it, but for me his words rang true in my search for something to kick-start our prayer at home. His phrase **"by heart"** resonated in me so resoundingly that I have adopted it as the theme of this book, in fact. For it is that phrase that I believe holds more than a grain of truth about what makes family prayer work. Basically, we have to pray together often enough that it becomes second nature to us. And we have to do it in relatively the same way all the time so that we can all begin to make the experience our own; so that we can do it **"by heart."**

This doesn't mean that it never changes or that we always say the same prayers, but it does mean that some things do remain the same. That sense of knowing what is going on is what makes traditions and rituals. If next Sunday night, for the first time ever, I call the family together in a darkened room, light a candle, read some scripture and sing a song, they are going to wonder what the heck is going on. Did someone die? Is Dad having a life crisis?

But if we do it again next week and the week after and the week after, they will begin to realise that – when I light the candle – something different and special is about to take place. That's what makes what we do a ritual. Pretty soon they will want to light the candle and read the readings and pray the prayers. And some Sunday night when I'm too tired to do it or I forget, it will be one of the kids who says, **"hey, why aren't we praying tonight?"** That's when our prayer has become tradition. And that's what this book is all about.

This book takes into consideration that no two families are alike. Yours may be a two-parent family and your chief concern may be passing on the prayers and beliefs of the Christian Church. You may be a single parent struggling with your own faith and yet still looking for ways to instil faith and a sense of spirituality in your children. You and your spouse may be of different faiths and are searching for ways to simply teach a basic understanding of God, Jesus, faith and the importance of prayer.

No one can create your family prayer traditions but you. What I do with my family may not work for yours. What this book aims to do is give you the means and the motivation to create your own rituals and build your own traditions.

First we'll look at the **"whys"** of family prayer and the motivating factors for establishing rituals and beginning traditions. Then I'll talk about the importance and meaning of ritual and give you ideas on how to create a family prayer tradition by explaining some of the elements that could play a part in your family's ritual.

Next we'll take a look at ways to celebrate special times like liturgical seasons and holy days. Finally, I'll give you some **"skeleton"** ideas for planning family devotions. They are skeletons because it is you who

9

must flesh them out and bring them to life within your families.

Along the way, I'll share with you some thoughts about family prayer traditions and some specific examples of some wonderfully creative ways that families have made their own traditions. I have been blessed with many friends who have been kind enough to share this part of their faith story for this book.

I want this book to be a starting point for you. As a matter of fact, I want it to be a starting place for me and my family, too. I'm no further along this road than you are, and I'll be experimenting along the way to see what works for us and what doesn't. It took nearly 2,000 years for the liturgy of the Church to evolve to where it is today. In the same way, developing rituals and traditions within our families takes time, experimentation, and a great desire to be together and share our faith. Only then will it come alive and be your own – something you can possess in your **"heart and mind and muscles."**

Chapter 1

What's In It For Me?

What's In It For Me?

Alex P. Keaton, Michael J. Fox's greed-loving television character on the American sitcom *"Family Ties"*, once sputtered:

> *"I'm not asking what's in it for me, I'm asking... what's in it for **me**?"*

Hopefully, we don't share Alex's insanely neurotic infatuation for money and possessions, but most of us – when we enter into a new relationship or join a new organisation – want to know how it is going to benefit us. We may not say that in so many words, but whether we're joining a church or a tennis club we want to know about the benefits of membership.

The same applies, in a much more subtle way, to our relationship with God. We go to church because we want to worship God, but we also go to church because it fulfils desires of our own – to be heard in prayer, to feel closer to God, to have a sense of community with those around us, to be at peace for one hour in the midst of a crazy world. So it's only natural and human to ask, as you consider beginning prayer traditions and praying with your families: ***"Why? Why should I do it? What will I get out of it? What will my family get out of it? Is it time well spent?"***

These are all good questions. Here are some of the ***"whys"*** of praying together as a family.

Building a Sense of Family

The truth is, many of us take our families for granted. We work hard at making business associates; we "network" and "schmooze" because it benefits our bottom line. We work hard at making and keeping friends because they nurture us as individuals and give us something to do at the weekends. But we often neglect our family because, after all, they are there whether we want them or not.

13

But that's not necessarily true. We all know people who haven't spoken to brothers or sisters or mothers or fathers for years because of ancient grudges often based on long-forgotten misunderstandings and arguments. And in an age where divorce is beginning to be more the norm and less the exception, no one can afford to take marriage and family for granted. Families, like our friends and our business associates, need to be nurtured.

If you think about when you became **"friends"** with your friends, you will realise that the solidification of that relationship into friendship had something to do with sharing – sharing an experience, sharing feelings, sharing an important moment. We don't become real friends just because we meet someone at a party. We become friends because we share something in common or we dare to drop our guard and share something personal about ourselves. We are friends because we know something of each other's true selves. If that never happens, we can never go beyond being waving acquaintances.

The same thing holds true for families. Why should there be any difference? If we just go through our domestic lives waving to each other as we walk out the door and never stop to talk and share and offer something of ourselves to the other members of the family, then we, too, will never go beyond being waving acquaintances. Familial relationships may produce loyalty to each other and a kind of **"he's my Dad so I love him"** love, but if you really want a family that will remain close and caring and loving, something else must be done to make that happen.

Praying together and sharing traditions is one way of creating that bond between family members. For once we share something so intimate, it can never be taken away and it leaves an indelible mark on each person and on the family as a whole.

As parents, it is our responsibility to create that bond. For it is the parents that set the tone of family life. Obviously, it's easier to begin something like a prayer tradition or ritual when your children are young. Trying to tie a teenager down for a 15-minute prayer session might be somewhat akin to trying to get a wild animal into a cage, unless they have been doing it with you for years and can't imagine their routine life without it. My friends Jim and Sue Russell write:

> **As with so many other facets of life** and ritual, it would seem to me that the key to family prayer is starting from day one and making prayer the ritual from the children's earliest memories.
>
> My family is a young and growing family (four children, ages 9,5,2, and 1, with one on the way), and if you were to ask our oldest, Jennifer, when we first began prayer as a family, she would certainly say she couldn't remember.
>
> Prayer at such tender ages may not be mature or meaningful from the adult standpoint, but a child in prayer – even a grinning one-year-old who sits down quietly and clasps her hands when she hears **"It's time for prayers!"**– can be a beautiful gesture of reverence to God.
>
> To have never known a time when the family DIDN'T stop as one and pray to God is a great gift and solid start of meaningful ritual. As they mature, so will the ritual, growing in meaning and fidelity to God.
>
> The grace of family prayer, like the graces of baptism, are perhaps best shared from the very beginning. Even the child in the womb is part of the circle of family prayer and certainly receives a measure of the graces bestowed on the prayerful family.

But don't despair if your children are older. If creating that all-important bond is important to you, then it's well worth your efforts. It may be harder going with older children, but even seemingly fruitless efforts with impatient teenagers may bear fruit years later when you watch them with their own children.

Passing on the Faith

Passing on the faith to our children always has been a concern and a source of frustration for Christian parents. And in an age of multimedia competition for our children's minds, hearts and souls, where can a parent start?

The obvious answer, of course, is at home. Whether you are interested in passing on the tenets of the Christian Church or simply an understanding of the love and caring of God, there is simply not a better place to begin than on your home turf. For when you pray at home, your actions are speaking louder than the words you are praying. You are saying to your children: **This is important to me. It's not just something I do on Sunday. My faith is an alive, active part of my life. It gives me power and it gives me peace. And I want you to have this, too.**

Religion is **"caught"** more than it's taught because what we do is always more powerful than what we say. If we scream **"don't scream!"** at our children, guess what they learn to do if they want to be heard? Likewise, if we say **"say your prayers"** or **"go to church"** and then do neither ourselves then we are fighting a losing battle. They will remember that we sat at home sipping coffee on Sunday morning while they went to church. They will remember us laughing with cocktails in our hands while we sent them off to say their bedtime prayers. In short, if they never see us at prayer, chances are they won't develop into praying adults. And although it's important that young people receive formal religious education, parents who think that education will ensure their child's faith are greatly overestimating the powers of even the best teachers and also are underestimating the impact they can have on their kids.

The most important thing that your child can see in you is a religious spirit and a stance toward life that makes God an active part. Despite what they sometimes say and do, they are watching and listening to us a lot more than they will ever let on.

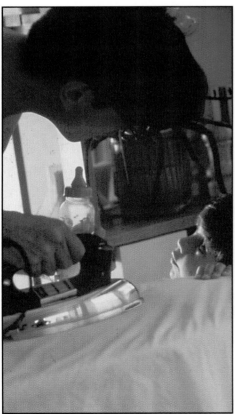
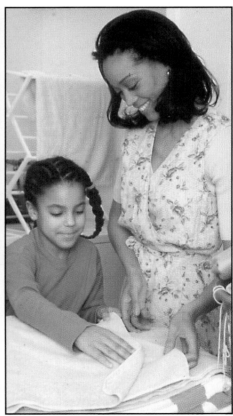

My mother taught me religion; my father taught me faith. My mother showed me the meaning of compassion; my father showed me the meaning of holiness. No, of course, it's not that simple; they did everything as a couple, including form my spirit.

I don't remember when I started joining my father for Perpetual Help devotions every Tuesday evening at 7.30pm – probably around five years old. Although it was just he and I walking across the street to church, it was a family ritual. Mum made sure I broke from homework in time, and the other kids never questioned where we were going.

The memories are clear and distinct. The smell of machine oil and iron shavings that no amount of Lava soap could remove from his hands. His unique and unrestrained baritone singing the hymns in the days when a man's voice was seldom heard in a Catholic church except from the altar or the choir-loft. **O Mother of Perpetual Help, To thee we come imploring help...'**

He was totally absorbed in the prayers, never glancing at the novena booklet, **'I love thee O most amiable Lady; and, for the love which I bear thee, I promise to serve thee always and to do all in my power to make others also love thee.'** A predominantly blue-collar, World War II veteran, male confraternity knelt for Benediction. **'O Salutaris Hostia, Quae caeli pandis ostium!'**

I treasure the memories and my Perpetual Help novena booklet; we should all treasure the power of a father's example of holiness.

Greg Christoffel

Nurturing Participative Christians

Passing on the faith and **"creating"** Catholics or Christians of other faiths is certainly a powerful incentive for bringing faith home. But of equal concern for many parents is not just **"filling the pews,"** but nurturing individuals who will take their faith seriously and practice it with a full heart, a loud voice, and a yearning soul. If getting them into church is all you want, a dose of good, old-fashioned guilt may do the trick. But is that what you want for your children?

Helping our children become active, worshiping Christians is not an easy task for one important reason: participation is not as essential to life in general as it once was. With each successive technological advancement, various aspects of our life become less and less participative. We **WATCH** television and we **LISTEN** to the radio. We experience adventure through the **"miracle"** of **"virtual reality,"** computers, and video games. So we **"virtually"** (but not really) engage in life. All this may add some needed enjoyment to our lives and entertain us, but it has also made us lazy. We don't want to **"do"**; we want to be **"done to."** We go to church to **"hear"** mass being **"said."**

Once people sat around the fire in a circle and told stories and sang songs with family and friends. Through those old traditions new generations learned the stories and songs of their families and communities. They became a tight-knit clan because they shared those things. And they learned how to tell stories, how to play instruments, how to sing songs. They learned what it means to be a member.

The same applies to our faith. We can go through our lives in virtual-reality mode – being "almost there" – or we can sit around the fire, learn the stories and songs of our faith and learn to be a member of the Christian family. Some of that learning takes place at church, but the real onus for passing on those traditions lies with parents.

So if we teach our children at home – whether sitting around the fire or the kitchen table – that prayer is key to our relationship with God, they will begin to learn at an early age how natural it is to raise their voices in praise, to take their cares to God in prayer, and to be a part of the nourishing community that is the Church.

Our family prayer life is pretty uncomplicated, but there are a few points to it that might be worth sharing. Grace before meals is something that's important to us; Christine usually sums up things that we might all be grateful for when she does it, and I'm more likely to recite the (slightly amended for inclusivity) grace from the Book of Common Prayer that borrows from Jewish tradition:

"Blessed are you, Ruler of the Universe, who gives us food to sustain our bodies and make our hearts glad, through Christ our Lord, Amen."

Bob & Christine Franke

Strengthening Family Communication

As parents, we sometimes either think we know what's going on in our children's lives (but don't) or we just don't want to know at all. On the other hand, just how much do our kids know about our lives? They know mum and dad either stay home or go to work during the day, but do they know our struggles and frustrations? Do they know of our concerns for them and the choices they make, or do they just hear us yell in exasperation when they don't make the right choices (in our humble opinions)?

Coming together for a time of family prayer can at times be a great forum for airing many of these concerns and more. (I would like to stress here, however, that family prayer and family communication sessions are not the same thing. Even if talking about important issues becomes a part of the prayer tradition, it's still important to do the talking within the context of prayer.) Part of the secret of creating

21

successful family prayer traditions is building an environment where honesty and respect are honoured.

For many years I helped run a youth group for teenagers in my parish church. We (the leadership team) built a relationship with these kids that enabled us to have lively, frank discussions on a wide range of issues. I know working with other people's kids is not the same as working with your own, but I believe the basic principles remain the same. They are:

> **EVERYONE MUST BE HONEST.** It's not fair encouraging the kids to be honest and then not doing the same. Letting them see your frustrations and pains is a powerful witness.

> **EVERYONE MUST LISTEN.** Pay absolute attention to the person talking and let them know that what they are saying is important. Get on their level. Sit down and listen. Look them in the eye.

> **EVERYONE DESERVES RESPECT.** Respect their honesty, even if what they are telling you is painful. If a serious issue is raised that must he handled with appropriate parental action, try not to do that during the time of prayer. Acknowledge their forthrightness, take it all to God in prayer, and then deal with them and the problem later.

In the youth group, we had one solid rule: whatever is said within the group stays within the group. I believe the same can hold true for the family. The children need to know you won't be talking about them, and what they say, to your friends and family.

Those are the most important principles. Here are a few others for creating effective family communication and family prayer traditions:

CHOOSE AN APPROPRIATE TIME to gather the family together. Don't suddenly announce on Saturday morning that "now we're going to pray," when children's minds are on football and friends.

CHOOSE AN APPROPRIATE PLACE where you won't be interrupted by telephones. Turn on the answering machine or just ignore the phone and don't let anything interrupt your prayer time. Your attitude toward this speaks louder than your words about the importance of prayer.

CHOOSE APPROPRIATE TOPICS for discussion. Start out with simple issues. Don't just jump in with sex and drug abuse. Talk about the highlights of each other's week, common interests and skills, friends and music. But don't just ask "How was school and what did you learn today?"

Connecting Faith to Life

If there is one dominant reason why people – young and old – leave the Church or give up on their faith, it is probably because they fail to find it relevant to their life. Indeed the ideas of a loving God watching over us and a forgiving Saviour eager to forgive can seem a distant reality when faced with mounting bills, sickness, and assorted other family troubles.

24

As parents concerned with passing on the faith, however, it is just these concerns that – when integrated into family prayer – can make faith and prayer and God all the more relevant to our young Christians. For when we share our worries and our problems with our children and with our God, our children see in us a faith born of fire. They see people of faith who come to God not just to say "thank you, keep us safe and please bless grandma," but to bring to God real concerns. What that says to the children is that faith is about real life and that it's important for survival.

Here are a few tips for helping your children see the relevance of prayer and faith:

> **Use family prayer time as an opportunity to deal with hard issues like death, divorce and other problems that affect families.**
>
> **Tell your children about things happening in your life right now and ask them what's happening in theirs.**
>
> **Tell your children how these things make you feel and ask about their feelings. Never negate their experience by telling them they were too young to feel a certain way, especially if they are talking about young love. You can save yourself a lot of trouble by not dismissing how another person feels.**
>
> **Tell your children how prayer helps you deal with these things.**
>
> **Don't be afraid to tell them that sometimes you forget to pray and take these things to God. Children don't need role models that are perfect, just ones that are honest and striving always to do better and make their faith stronger.**

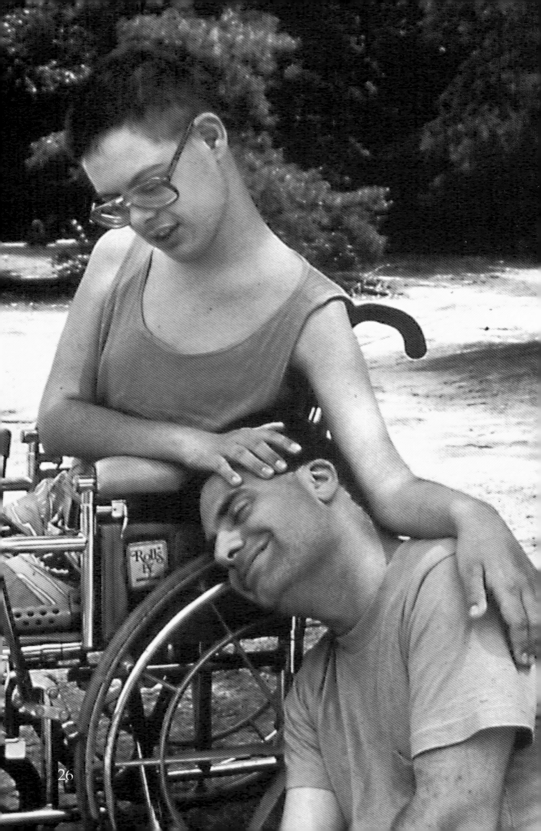

Establishing and Reinforcing Christian Values

My father-in-law once told me (or perhaps more than once) that when faced with a difficult decision, he tries to ask himself: **"What would Jesus have done?"** That's a simple enough question, but I think it cuts to the quick. For isn't that the kind of questioning of motives that we would like to instil in our children?

We live during a time when just the term **"family values"** or **"Christian values"** can produce a sneer in a group of people. Christians, with their supposed **"simple"** solutions to difficult problems, are the butt of jokes. But no one (not even Jesus) said being a Christian was going to be easy. If we're going to call ourselves Christians, then it's important to act and live and make decisions in ways that reflect the teachings of Christ. It's not easy and it's not popular, but if we say we're Christians then we have to live the part.

How can we learn to turn the other cheek instead of hitting back? We have to learn not to steal and covet and kill. We need to learn how to apply these teachings to all the various aspects of our lives. It is important to ask ourselves **"What would Jesus have done?"** But be warned: your children will be watching you far more than they will be listening to you. You can tell them to turn the other cheek and forgive, but if you don't, well .... you know what they're going to remember.

During your times of family prayer, especially during those times when you're dealing with difficulties, taking time to instil these kinds of values will seem natural. Acknowledging that you wanted to hit someone because they made you angry may be healthy for you and for your children. We're all human and we're going to have those kinds of feelings. But far more important is to show and tell them how you didn't hit the person and how you went to them later and settled the situation in a Christ-like way. Your children will remember that forever.

Strengthening Personal Faith

Finally, one of the most important benefits of creating and maintaining family prayer traditions is that they will nourish your own faith. I've been talking about the importance of nurturing your children's faith, but it is important to look after yourself as well.

Our jobs, our house chores, our volunteer work, and – yes – our children, all take us to the brink of insanity at times. As adults, and especially as parents, our lives are so often focused on others that we don't make the time for ourselves and God. If it's been a while since you've spent time with God in uninterrupted prayer, perhaps beginning a prayer tradition with your family is one step in the right direction toward recreating that relationship. And when we speak and pray with our children about such things as building family, the importance of faith, being participative Christians, connecting faith to life, and living with Christian values, we are, of course, reinforcing all those values and ideas in our own lives.

Chapter 2

Creating Your Own Rituals and Traditions

Creating Your Own Rituals and Traditions

For many people, the word ritual may call to mind stark, mindless ceremonies. For some it may even have the dark, evil connotation of satanic ritual. Neither of those, of course, is what I'm talking about.

For others, the word may hold no negative meaning but may still evoke images of candles, incense and ancient ceremonies. And while your family rituals may be performed by candlelight, that's still not the meaning of ritual that is most important to understand. Here is an example of the kind of ritual that is more symbolic of what I'm trying to get at:

*"**We share memorised prayer** at mealtimes and participate in liturgies throughout the week, but the time for spontaneous prayer comes at night before the boys go to bed. We all lay on our bed (it's the biggest) and begin by reciting the "**Now I Lay Me Down to Sleep**" prayer followed by "**Father, we thank you for the gift of this day,**" and then we each take turns saying the things that happened to us that day (large and small) for which we are grateful. For example, they may say, '**thank you for the beautiful weather, for being able to play soccer with our friends, for the great barbecued chicken we had for dinner, for jumping on the trampoline, for finding my favourite ball I thought I'd lost, for having pony ride day at school, etc.'***

We always end with 'Thank you for our families and friends who love us so much.' We find this to be a very positive way to end the day, to recognise how very blessed we are, and to instil in our sons an attitude of gratitude."

Larry & Dianne G'Sell

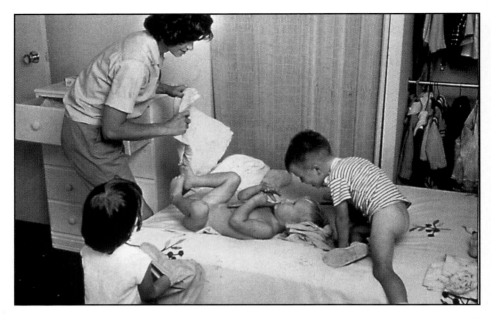

In this simple "ritual" are many of the keys to what makes ritual ritual and what makes ritual work. Let's take a closer look...

There is a set time for the ritual.

"The time for spontaneous prayer comes at night before the boys go to bed..."

Ritual needs to be an expected thing. The key word used throughout Larry and Dianne's story is **always**. We **always** do this. That doesn't mean you can never be flexible, but it does mean that it works best when we (and especially children) know when to expect it. I have no doubt that if Dianne and Larry were ever to forget to pray with the boys they would be quickly reminded. **Before bedtime** is a good time to pray, especially with younger children, because it is probably the quietest time of the day.

Mealtime is another good time, for it is generally a time when the whole family gathers together. Simply beginning each meal by saying grace is a tradition worth beginning and maintaining in our families. But it is also possible to transform entire meals into prayer traditions by using that time together to share thoughts on life's blessings and troubles. Jesus obviously knew the power of sharing a meal together.

So unless your kids are different from mine, trying to coral them all together to pray before they shoot out the door in the morning would be a fruitless exercise. It's important to find the best time for your family and then stick to it.

There is a set pattern to the prayer.

"We all lay on the bed".

First we do this and then we do this. Then we end by doing this. There is comfort in what we know well and "by heart." Dianne and Larry's four boys know the routine. They know what's expected of them. They know when the prayer starts, what comes in the middle and how it ends. They don't need to have it in a book and there's nothing to memorise because it has become a part of their everyday life. Does that make it mindless? Absolutely not. Some things we just have to learn to do without thinking because they are good for us. We wash our hands before we eat. We brush our teeth after every meal.

We look both ways before crossing the street. Shouldn't prayer become that kind of necessity in our lives? Shouldn't we teach our children that it is?

Ritual is participative.

Whether you recite "Now I Lay Me Down to Sleep" or share the blessings of your life in a more spontaneous way, what you do together as a family should involve the whole family. When the children see mum or dad praying it sets a good example and tells them that prayer is not just a thing for children. Sending children off to bed with the clarion call of "say your prayers" is not family prayer. Pray with them. Give them that time.

Prayer will really become meaningful and essential for children only when they are allowed substantial, meaningful participation in it. Letting an older child light a candle or read the scripture is not just a nice gesture, it's imperative. And, as Dianne and Larry's example shows, it's important that the children get their say. Allowing them to talk about their day and their successes, failures and blessings allows them to make that important connection between faith and life. God is not just about our eternal salvation (although God certainly is that). God is about the here and now.

Ritual is meaningful.

We pray with our children because it has meaning for them and us:

"We find this to be a very positive way to end the day, to recognise how very blessed we are, and to instil in our sons an attitude of gratitude."

That's why the G'Sells do it, although the boys won't tell you that they like to pray because it "instils in them an attitude of gratitude." But because they pray every night they are ever mindful of the blessings in their life, and they know from whom those blessings flow. They are grateful to God, but they might not be if they didn't lay on that bed every night and think about it.

Why Ritual Is Important

A ritual is a special act that links people through shared meaning. For years, anthropologists and psychologists have been trying to figure out what makes a certain group of people a **"people."** Ritual provides a part of that answer.

B est-selling author Robert Fulghum wrote in his book *"From Beginning to End"* that ceremonies and celebrations for births, deaths, marriages and reunions are how we **"change yet remain constant from one stage of life to another."** Ritual is also how we (as a family or as a culture) remain the same from generation to generation. In the case of prayer traditions, ritual is how we pass on our faith to our children, for rituals affect families the way that everyday life cannot. It is, in fact, because they are not ordinary that they **"work."** A ritual slows us down from our busy lives and says: take your time right now. What you are doing is important and meaningful. When we turn off the television and gather the children in a circle or on the bed, they know something has changed. They know something special is happening– even if you do it everyday.

Established rituals can also ease the pain in times of personal loss. Deaths, divorces, family moves and the like can all be dealt with within the framework of prayer.

For example, soon after we moved to England, we heard of the death of Angie, a teenage girl who was a member of the church youth group and who also baby-sat for our family on occasion. Being so far away from the sad reality of that, we had never got around to telling our eight-year-old son, Jon, who knew Angie well. We finally found a way to do that within our family prayer ritual. He was still sad, of course, but we were able to help him turn his grief into prayer for Angie's soul and for her family.

Likewise, two of our closest friends back in the States had been struggling in their marriage for sometime and had finally agreed to divorce. We didn't know how to tell Jon, who was very close to both of them. I know we wanted to protect him from the pain and the confusion, but we still needed to let him know. Doing that during our prayer time allowed us all to pray for them and for our own family. It also allowed us to talk together about the importance of family and marriage and to affirm to ourselves and to our children that our family was in good shape.

Flexibility

I was at a meeting once when an organisational consultant told the group that we should be **"rigid in our pursuit of flexibility."** It brought a laugh to the group, but there's a lot of truth in his words. For even though I have advocated the importance of creating rituals at set times with set patterns, it is just as important to remain flexible in the way you approach family prayer. Rituals can lose their power if they are adhered to too tightly and become inflexible in their form and scheduling. It's nice to say **"we're going to pray together every night for 15 minutes,"** but if that becomes a burden and a **"groaning"** experience for some or all involved, it might be better and more productive to schedule one evening together each week or keep the schedule open and flexible. Only you can discern that within your own family.

Furthermore, many traditions may need to grow and mature along with your children. What worked when they were five probably won't work when they are fifteen. Will Dianne and Larry still be able to gather all the boys on their bed when they have four teenagers? Probably not. But that doesn't mean they can't gather around the table or the fire. So although some rituals may come and go as children grow up, over a period of years you will come to learn what are the most important and meaningful elements of your family's prayer rituals. The prayers may change, the setting may change but – for example – your children may stubbornly refuse (and rightly so) to begin a ritual without lighting the special prayer candle or reciting a certain prayer.

What's most important is that years from now the G'Sell boys will most probably be lying in bed with their own children listening to them pray. That's passing on the faith and that's the power of ritual and tradition.

The Elements of Your Ritual

The key to family prayer tradition, as I have been emphasising, is to create one yourself. You may have traditions from your own childhood that you would like to pass on to your children. You may choose to change those old traditions and make them new for your own children. You may have ideas of your own or may have heard of traditions that you think might work with your family.

But you may feel like you don't know how or where to start. So, in addition to some of the suggestions I've already given you, in this next section I want to give you some ideas that you might be able to apply to your own families. If something looks good, try it out. If it doesn't work, throw it out or change it to meet your needs and the personality of your family. Like telling a good story, a good ritual has a beginning, a middle and an end, and once you begin to establish a way that you "do" your ritual, you're on your way to establishing a tradition that may last for generations.

Beginning the Ritual

How you begin your ritual is important because it sets the tone for what is to follow. It is for this reason that we don't just walk into church, go up to the altar and receive communion. Instead, we have to prepare ourselves for that special moment. So we pray, we sing, we light the candles, we spend time in silence and ask God for forgiveness. Then we listen to God's word. Then we prepare the gifts. Then we receive communion.

If you simply call the children into a room, sit them down and say, "Okay, let's pray about what's happening in your life," you might get no response at all. They – and you – need a little time to "get in the mood" to pray, which is why it's important to begin the ritual effectively. Here are some ideas for kicking off your prayer time together. They can be used in combination, of course:

> **turn out the lights**
> **pray silently for five minutes**
> **light a candle**
> **sing a song**
> **light a fire in the fireplace**
> **listen to a song**
> **burn incense**
> **hold hands**
> **exchange hugs**
> **sit quietly and write down what you want to pray for, what you're sorry for, etc.**

The Middle

Once you're relaxed and have made some sort of transition from the hectic pace of life to the slowed-down time of family prayer, it's time for the "meat," so to speak, of your family prayer. Remember, one of the keys to ritual is that it is meaningful. Our prayer time together must reflect something of our faith. It must instil in us and our children a sense of a loving God who truly cares for us, otherwise it's just "family time." That is, certainly, good in itself, but it's not what prayer is about and it will do little to pass our faith and beliefs on to our children.

There are limitless ideas of what you can do during this time, but here are a few ideas:

> **scripture readings or readings from a daily reflection book**
>
> **poems and other readings, including those written by you or your children**
>
> **recited, memorised prayers like the Our Father, the Hail Mary, the Rosary**
>
> **spontaneous prayers (what I'm thankful for, what I'm sorry about, what I'm worrying about, prayers for the sick)**
>
> **singing songs**
>
> **listening to a song performed by a family member or on a recording**
>
> **talking and listening about the events of the day, problems, issues**
>
> **sharing a meal or a special treat while discussing for what you are thankful**
>
> **making something together while talking (a craft, a cake, biscuits**
>
> **preparing food for the local food pantry or homeless shelter while discussing our responsibilities as Christians**
>
> **reading the newspaper together and offering prayers for those you read about**

Wanting your children to "pray spontaneously" and getting them to do that can be two different things at times. But there are ways to make that process easier.

Pass the candle.

This is a tradition I started with the youth group and then later moved into our family prayer time. Simply sit in a circle and pass a candle from person to person. As the candle comes to you you have two options: you can pray out loud for whatever is on your mind and in your heart, or you can simply hold the candle and pray quietly for a few moments. Either way, everyone is involved.

Write down your prayers.

If some family members are shy about praying out loud, try this: have everyone write down their prayers on small slips of paper and then collect them in a basket. Then take turns drawing slips out of the basket and reading them. Or, you can just leave them in the basket as "silent" prayer requests and offer the whole basket up to God in prayer. You can even collect the slips in a fire-proof bowl or wok , burn the prayers, and watch the smoke float heavenward. If there's already a fire in the fireplace, just throw the slips in the fire and watch your cares and worries burn away.

Likewise, there is an art to facilitating meaningful discussions in which everyone is encouraged – but not mandated – to take part.

> **Ask open-ended questions that can't be answered with yes and no.**
>
> **Follow-up answers with more probing questions and try to explore the feelings behind the emotions.**
>
> **Encourage the use of "I" messages, especially if you're dealing with a conflict between family members. That means instead of saying "He always does this" or "she did that to me," you should try to turn those statements around to reflect how the person talking is feeling. So it becomes: "I feel angry and put on when he always does this" and "I felt really stupid when she did that to me."**
>
> Pass the conch. In the classic novel "The Lord of the Flies," the boys passed a conch shell to designate who was doing the talking so they all wouldn't talk at once. It doesn't have to be a conch shell, but sometimes it is useful to have something that says "I'm talking now and you have to listen."

Once a tradition is established, you'll find that the children will begin bringing their own ideas to the experience. They may have read a prayer or a story at church or school that they want to share. They may know a new song they want to teach or may just want to share with you (and with God) a new song on the piano or the violin or the tuba. They will want to pray for sick pets, friends and relatives.

42

Just remember it's important not to censor their contributions. Listen to the tuba solo with an open heart and, if they read a 15-minute story and you don't get the point, just ask them why they chose to read it. They may have a "good" reason, but they may just shake their heads and say, "because I really thought it was a good story." That's a good enough answer.

Ending the Ritual

Like beginning a ritual, it's important to do something special to mark the end of the prayer time. It may be as simple as blowing out the candle or reciting the same prayer. Many of the potential elements I listed for beginning a ritual (holding hands, exchanging hugs, singing a song) can be used to end your family prayer time. How you choose to end your ritual will be up to you and your family, but as in all elements of ritual, it's good to eventually decide on something meaningful and then do it all the time.

The Beauty of Ritual

The beauty of ritual is that it's there to help you. Imagine what would happen if every Sunday the priest would have to create a new way of doing the liturgy. Chaos would reign and nobody would be happy. But instead, the Church has an established ritual that, while allowing for flexibility and an abundance of new ideas, also creates a comfortable place we can all come because we "know the routine." We're at ease because we know what comes at the beginning and the middle and the end, and so we can tune in all the more closely to what's being said and done.

That's what establishing a ritual for your family can do. Instead of worrying about "how" we're going to do prayer tonight, you can relax, do what you always do, and then see what new thoughts and experiences are brought to that moment by you and your family. That's beautiful and that's the power of God moving among us.

Chapter 3

Holy Days and Holidays

Holy Days and Holidays

Traditionally, holidays and holy days existed to give us a chance to slow down a bit from the hectic pace of our daily lives and celebrate together as family. However, in an age where Christmas and the time leading up to it sometime mean little more than one party after another, and where Easter has been largely reduced to chocolate bunnies and coloured eggs, holy days and holidays are seldom seen as a break and the celebration has far more to do with gifts than sacred occasions.

Even when we **"get away"** and travel on our holidays, often those times can be filled with rushing from one destination and tourist attraction to the next. But even given all this, there are ways to make the most of these special family times together. For the family committed to spending time together in prayer, even the busiest times of the year can provide a needed respite.

Advent and Christmas

Perhaps the best way to turn the Christmas season into a time of family prayer is to start early – with Advent. Advent exists as a holy season separate from Christmas because we need that special time of preparation for the celebration of the extraordinary event of the birth of Christ. To experience Christmas fully, the Church knows we need that extra time to get ready.

So for the family wanting to pray more together, Advent is actually a great time to start. It's a way of saying to our children: **"We all know how busy we can be during this time leading up to Christmas, but it's important that we take the time to do this."** Advent also has some **"built-in rituals"** – like lighting a family advent wreath – that make it an ideal time to concentrate on family prayer.

47

But how you structure your family prayer time together during Advent is how you begin to build tradition. Just **"how"** you light the advent wreath and buy the Christmas tree and decorate the house and place the manger under the tree will determine what gets repeated from year to year. The details of how you do all these things are nearly as important as the fact that you do them at all. Details are what make traditions. It is **"how"** we do it, year after year, that creates feelings of belonging and ownership. Before long we begin to say things like: **"This is the way we always do it. This is our family tradition."** Some family traditions may be decades old. Some may be only a few years. But the important thing that happens within family traditions is that everyone has a stake in how they are carried out. I received this letter from my friend *Maleen Corrigan:*

I love family prayer traditions, and we have several that are an integral part of "who" the Corrigans are. One that I love most is a process.

At Christmas, after the advent wreath is *"finished"* I save the four purple candles remnants. In January, when we take the tree down, one of the boys takes it outside and saws a four- to eight-inch piece from the base. (When the children were little Jim or I did it, but we all went out to hold the tree). I then put the *"log"* away with the candles and wait for lent.

A few days before Ash Wednesday, we get it out and go to the basement to drill a 3/4" hole into the tree-piece to receive a candle. (For us, the drilling is especially meaningful, because we use a heavy, old, brace drill that belonged to my grandpa, and we always talked about him and my Dad, who are both dead.) Next we put the candle and a cactus and some rocks we have collected over the years on the dinner table. Every night during Lent, we have dinner by that candle light.

On Easter, I put a tall white candle in the log and replace the cactus with little spring flowers. It is a nice way of uniting Advent to Christmas to Lent to Easter – the crib to cross to new life. When the kids were little, we talked about that whole concept each year and now, when I start to talk about the symbol, they just sort of roll their eyes and say, *"We know, Mum."* And, the truth is, they really do.

So what the Corrigans have developed over the years is a finely tuned tradition that not only unites important Christian holy days but also unites several generations of the family, both living and dead. Would it matter if they used a brand-new cordless drill instead of the old brace drill that belonged to Maleen's grandfather and father? You bet it would. That detail (how to drill the hole) in itself is insignificant. But it becomes essential to the Corrigan family tradition. That's the secret of creating and maintaining family traditions – finding the details that make the ritual essential and meaningful to your family.

There are many, many books on the market designed to help your family celebrate Advent and prepare for Christmas. These books are a good way to get ideas to begin your family tradition.

49

Christmas eve and Christmas day provide another great opportunity for creating family traditions and rituals. In the midst of the busy-ness of Christmas, it is imperative that Christian families set apart time to pray together and thank God for the gift of his son. It's important to remember that – in many families – Christmas may come and go with no mention at all of the origins of our celebration. Sadly, this can even happen in **"Christian"** families. We're all busy and some families simply find it hard to talk about God and Jesus.

But even the simplest of traditions – such as reading the Christmas story from Luke's gospel, placing the infant Jesus in the manger or going to church together – can help instil faith and wonder in hearts both young and old. Christmas is already a magical time of year. With a little effort, it can also be a time for creating close family ties and nurturing our own faith and that of our children.

Lent and Easter

Like Advent and Christmas, the season of Lent and the celebration of Easter give us more opportunities to pray as a family, just as the Church as a whole commits itself to increased prayer and sacrifice during this special time of preparation. Lent is, of course, a more solemn time of year than Advent. We are called to introspection during these weeks leading up to Christ's passion, to thinking about our failings and about God's grace for us.

It's important to give our children (and show them by our own example) an example of the introspective person, to show them how essential it is to take a close look at ourselves and the way we live our lives. The most powerful example we can give, of course, is to say to them: **"This is how I have failed. These are the things I need to learn to do better. These are the things I'm sorry for."** This kind of example goes much further and deeper into their hearts and minds than **"Dad has given up beer for Lent."**

Lent is also a time during which we are called to increase our good works and our compassion and action for those in need. So it can be a natural extension of family prayer time to work together as a family to meet some of those needs. Preparing sandwiches for the local food pantry and helping your elderly neighbours with chores are strong **"prayers"** that take faith and prayer out of the abstract and into the real world. For our children, there can be no better lesson in the responsibilities of being a Christian.

Surrounding these helping experiences with prayer and discussion helps solidify the experience and makes a concrete connection between faith and life, especially for young children. They need to understand that we care for others not just because it's a good thing to do, but because it's what we are asked to do by Jesus. It's part and parcel of being a Christian, not an elective experience.

As Lent ends and the joy of Easter comes, it's essential to make that same transition in your family prayer. In my wife's family, the established tradition is attending church together on Easter

Saturday so we can all break our Lenten fasts together. If you gave up ice cream for Lent, all the ice cream you want is waiting for you at the party. But it's not just a reward for keeping your Lenten promise, it's a celebration of the new life that Christ offers us in his resurrection.

Just as with the celebration of Christmas day, it is essential that families take the time to recall the real meaning of Easter. In the rush of Easter baskets, egg hunts, and trips to Grandma's house, it is sometimes easy to forget to tell the story of the resurrection and talk about its importance to us. Perhaps most importantly we need to take the time to say thank you to God for the gift of life – our life, the life around us, and the promise of eternal life to come.

Connecting Family to Parish Life

Our family traditions are really bound up in our parish family traditions, and this feels really good to me. Christine my wife, Elizabeth my fourteen-year-old daughter, and I all sing in the choir together, and the parish feels like home to us at this point – *"not as a stranger or a guest, but like a child at home,"* to quote the old hymn.

The parish acts as at least part of an extended family, although our birth families live far away. It has supported our little nuclear family in many ways, and its traditions are not the least of that support.

Bob Franke

Bob makes an important point when he says, **"Our family traditions are really bound up in our parish family traditions."** For when we pray at home, we are not replacing the important acts of praise and worship that take place within the larger body of Christ that is the local church. In fact, there is a real danger in establishing prayer traditions within our homes if we are establishing them to replace going to church.

Rather, our family prayer should complement and connect to what we learn and receive from our parish. What we hear in church on Sunday or what our children learn at school or religion classes should all feed into the celebrations and the prayers and the discussions that take place at home within the **"domestic Church."**

Simply going to church together on Sunday and on other holy days is an act of family worship. A worshipping family is a strong, clear witness to the rest of the world that says, in the words of Joshua, **"as for me and my house, we will serve the Lord."** It is evangelisation by example, and it is a message to those around us that comes with responsibility. For when our friends, co-workers and neighbours know that we go to church, we are instantly held up to higher standards than those who do not. So when we act in un-Christ-like ways, we may immediately be held up as hypocrites: **"Yeah, they may go to church every week, but look at the way they act."**

On the other hand, if we try earnestly to show our Christian commitment by the way we live, that, too, will be observed. My mother – who was not a regular church-goer later in her life – always liked to refer to one particular family in our church – the Challs – whom she thought really lived their faith. That was the kind of faith she wanted me to have. The way we act as Christians does get noticed.

Hello Jon,

I meant to write to you before you left on your trip about your First Communion. I remember my First Communion very well considering how many years it's been. Over fifty. WOW! You made me remember how important that day was to me. It was the first time I remember feeling close to God. It was a relationship that meant so much in my life. There were many times when things didn't seem to go like I thought they should and the way I thought that God would allow them to go. But we find that God often has a hidden plan that we sometimes don't understand. As we go along we need to know that God loves us and one of the ways that we feel God's love is when He acts through us. His love grows in us everyday and one of the best ways I know to nourish that love is through the sacraments, especially Holy Communion. That is the time when I most feel God tugging on my heart and reminding me how he loves me and wants me to share that love with my family, friends and all those we meet in our daily lives. Everyday I ask God to watch over you and keep you close to Him. The world can be a tough place and we need our Super-hero, Jesus, to show us the way. So always stay close to Him and remember every time you go to Communion to ask Jesus for His help. He and Grandpa love you very much.

your soccer buddy,
Grandpa

We "get" our faith from church, but it needs to be nurtured and fed at home. True, strong, faith – the kind that people will point to – is the kind that is lived day-in and day-out, whether we're at home or at church. Praying as a family helps to build that kind of faith.

Furthermore, how we as families celebrate "Christian milestones" like First Communion and Confirmation says a lot to our children about the importance of these events. My son received his First Communion last year following a year of intense "family" preparation for the event. He went to school every week, and my wife and I went to monthly parents meetings and together the whole family participated in monthly celebrations at the parish for the First Communion class. At home, we talked about what he was learning in his classes and tried to reinforce those lessons with prayer and discussion about the importance of the Eucharist. When the day finally arrived it really felt like a family event, even though it was his special day.

Ask him now what presents he received that day and he probably won't know, but he'll remember the letter he received from his grandfather back in America. The letter shows the power and meaningfulness of connecting family to church, and I hope it is a tradition – started with his first grandchild – that my father-in-law will continue with the rest of the clan.

Holidays

Finally, family holidays can give families the opportunities to **"retreat and re-treat"** as a retreat director once said to me. When we go on holiday we **"retreat"** from our daily lives and immerse ourselves in a different schedule, a different place, and perhaps even a different culture. We get away from everything that is normal and live differently for a while. But during those times away we also need to **"re-treat"** our lives; to give some needed attention to our spiritual selves.

Long car drives and nights at the self-catering cottage are both wonderful opportunities to put some perspective in our lives and pray and discuss issues that are burning within us but haven't had time to come out. It's also a good time to count our blessings and say thank you for all we have been given, including the holiday itself.

Here are a few suggestions for making holidays into mini-retreats without throwing the kids into a revolution:

> **Talk over meals about the new things your family is experiencing while on holiday and try to connect those experiences with issues of faith.**
>
> **Attend church together and visit other sites of religious significance like old churches, cathedrals and monasteries.**
>
> **Say a prayer when you see the inevitable road accidents.**
>
> **Begin and end each day with a short prayer.**

Chapter 4

Family Devotion Ideas

Family Devotion Ideas

How to use this section

This section of the book is designed to give you a starting place for regular, themed, family devotions. The following pages give you 20 different ideas for prayer sessions and provide suggested prayers, readings and questions and actions to stir thoughts and imaginations.

Still, it's up to you to provide the "details" of your own family ritual that will transform this time together with your family into a tradition. How you begin and end your ritual (see chapter 2) and how you choose to adapt the material provided is what makes tradition. Be creative, and be open to ideas from all members of the family. Try out different ideas and see what works and what doesn't. In the early days of your time praying together, be particularly attentive to responses. Quickly some elements of your ritual will become essential and meaningful, and those will be the beginning of lasting traditions.

Family

SUGGESTED READINGS:

Genesis 2: 18-24
(The creation of the first family)

Luke 2: 1-20
(The Christmas story)

1 Corinthians 13:1-13
(The gift of love)

Colossians 3:12-21
(Christian behaviour)

REFLECTION:

"How's the family?" is a common enough question, but often we reply with the old standard: "Fine. Everyone's healthy." But it's good to reflect once in a while on just how "fine" the family is and to thank God for all the blessings we receive as family. For it is very often those closest to us who get the smallest pieces of our attention, understanding, forgiveness and love. Our families are pure gifts from God, but like so many gifts we receive, families and the relationships within them are often ignored, disregarded, abused and, at the worst of times, discarded and forgotten. Spend some time now reflecting on the blessings of your family and talking together about how your family could be made stronger.

THINK ABOUT...

● What's so important about a family?
● What's the best thing about being a part of your family?
● Are there misunderstandings and grudges within your family that need to be cleared up?
● Do you need to ask forgiveness for anything from someone in your family?
● Say what you love best about each member of your family.
● Exchange hugs as signs of peace and love.

TALK ABOUT...

CONCLUDING PRAYER:

Bless our family, Lord, and keep us all safe. Thank you for our family and for all the wonderful things you give to us. Help us to love each other more and be patient with each other. Slow us down, Lord. Show us the wounds that need to be healed. Uncover our eyes to the misunderstandings that need to be clarified. Guide us to the grudges that need to be thrown away. Hear us now as we pray. Amen.

Forgiveness

REFLECTION:

How do we approach forgiveness within our families? Or do we at all? Often it is more convenient to just sweep problems and arguments under the carpet and pretend that they never happened. However, as Christians we are called to both forgive and forget. And just as Jesus both washed feet and allowed his feet to be washed, we are asked by God to forgive and allow others to forgive us. Problems swept under the carpet never go away until they are taken out and forgiven. If the relationships within our families are precious to us, they deserve the same type of forgiveness and unconditional love that God offers to his children. It's a tough model to follow but it's worth the effort.

SUGGESTED READINGS:

Mark 11:20-25
(Forgive and you will be forgiven)

2 Chronicles 7:12-16
(A promise of forgiveness)

Matthew 6:9-15
(The Lord's Prayer)

Matthew 18:21-35
(The parable of the unforgiving debtor)

Luke 6:36-38
(Be compassionate)

THINK ABOUT...

- What does it mean to forgive someone?
- Why is it important for us to forgive others?
- When was the last time you forgave someone?
- When was the last time you were forgiven?
- Tell each other member of your family one thing for which you are sorry.
- Write things you are sorry for on a piece of paper. Collect the papers and burn them in an ash tray, symbolising God's forgiveness.

TALK ABOUT...

CONCLUDING PRAYER:

Forgive us, Lord, for the times we are too stubborn to forgive. Thank you for the gift of your unconditional love. Thank you for the loving people in our family who are quick to forgive us when we go wrong. Most of all, thank you, Lord, for the many times you forgive us, and thank you for Jesus, whose death took away all our sins. Hear us now as we pray. Amen.

61

Communication

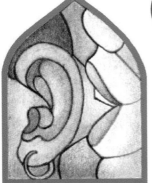

SUGGESTED READINGS:

Isaiah 40:21-26
(Understanding by seeing and hearing)

Genesis 11:1-9
(The tower of Babel)

Luke 24:13-35
(The Road to Emmaus)

Acts 2:1-13
(Pentecost)

REFLECTION:

We talk all the time. We talk at each other and over each other and at times – it seems – straight through each other. But do we take the time to talk to one another, sharing what's most important in our lives and listening to the important things that the others in our family have to say? That's a tougher go. It should be easy to communicate within a family because of the close relationships that already exist. But instead, often just the opposite happens. We become so used to each other that we just don't pay attention to what's going on and being said around us. That's why we need to slow down once in a while and really talk and listen. As a family, we deserve that time.

THINK ABOUT...

- When did you last talk too much?
- When did you last not listen enough?
- Do you feel others in your family listen to you?
- Do you feel you can have your say within your family?
- Say what the three most important things in your life are.
- Complete this sentence: "What I want you to understand about me is..."

TALK ABOUT...

CONCLUDING PRAYER:

Lord, help us to communicate more clearly with each other. Give us patience and a loving heart so we can listen to what others are saying and respect the way they feel. Give us the power to always communicate clearly to the rest of the world how important you are to us. Give us ears that can hear and eyes that can see those people around us who need our love and compassion. Hear us now as we pray. Amen.

Prayer

REFLECTION:

When children call out in the middle of the night, they know their call will be answered. They have faith that their parents will answer their cry. In the same way, God hears all of us when we call out for him. Like a loving parent, he is there to soothe our troubles. When we pray, do we really expect an answer, just as the child knows he or she will be heard and comforted? Praying to God is an act of faith, but we're only half way there if we don't truly believe we're going to have our prayers answered. In the scriptures, again and again Jesus tells his disciples of the power of prayer and urges them on – by word and by his own example – to seek God in the solace of prayer.

SUGGESTED READINGS:

Matthew 6:5-15
(Jesus teaches us how to pray)

Ephesians 6:10-20
(Put on the armour of Christ)

Luke 11:9-13
(Ask and it shall be given)

Luke 18:1-8
(Pray continually)

Matthew 18:19-20
(Prayer in common)

THINK ABOUT...

- Do you believe God answers prayers?
- How does God answer prayers?
- Discuss this: God always answers prayers, but sometimes his answer is "no."
- Tell about a time when a prayer was answered.
- Share with your family the people and things for whom you want to pray.

TALK ABOUT...

CONCLUDING PRAYER:

Lord, teach us how to pray and give us the faith to expect an answer. Help us to understand that you are there for us like a loving, watchful, ever-listening parent. Open our eyes to all that is happening around us so we can recognise you working in our lives and answering our prayers. Hear all our prayers, Lord, those that we have the courage to speak out loud and those that we keep hidden in our hearts. Hear us now as we pray. Amen.

Faith

REFLECTION:

Faith is a fire within us that at times smoulders and at other times burns with intensity. Sometimes we may feel very faithful and faith-filled, while at other times we doubt the significance and meaning of our faith. Faith is not an easy thing, for in faith we set aside the rational and the reasonable and throw our lot in with a loving – but invisible – God who offers us a life of hope and love. God is the sure gentle hand within us, leading us to faith and the fullness of life. But we can't prove that to anyone else. It has to be taken "on faith." To those without faith, we may appear simple-minded or even crazy. But we know we have been touched by his hand and scorched by his fire.

SUGGESTED READINGS:

Matthew 9: 1-7
(Cure of a paralytic)

Matthew 14:22-34
(Jesus walks on water)

Genesis 6:1-22
(Noah and the ark)

Daniel 6:11-24
(Daniel in the lion's den)

THINK ABOUT...

- When is our faith strongest?
- When is it weakest?
- What can we do to strengthen our faith?
- Tell about a time when your faith really made a difference in your life.
- Tell about a time when someone else's faith affected you.

TALK ABOUT...

CONCLUDING PRAYER:

We pray and ask you to strengthen our faith and the faith of the world, O Lord. Through our works and actions, may others come to see the power of faith and witness the difference that a life centred on you makes. Help us to show our faith by living each day for you alone. May our faith change our lives and the lives of those around us. Thank you for the gift of our faith. Hear us now as we pray. Amen

Hope

REFLECTION:

Hope is what separates us from despair. As Christians, our hope in Christ is not a hope that we muster inside ourselves like courage or bravado, but instead it is a hope that calls upon a power that we cannot even begin to fathom. When teenagers talk about the decisions and pressures they face, they very often frame those issues with either a sense of hope or an absence of hope. With hope, with a sense of something larger in their life beyond the moment, they can see beyond the moment when somebody offers them drugs and beyond the moment of feeling that their life is so meaningless that they might as well take their own life. But without hope, we are all easy prey for the pressures of the world.

SUGGESTED READINGS:

Romans 8: 18-25
(Glory is our hope)

1 Corinthians 13:1-13
(Faith, hope and love)

2 Corinthians 3:4-18
(Confidence through Christ)

Galatians 5:1-6
(Liberty in Christ)

THINK ABOUT...

- What is your biggest hope in life?
- How does faith in Christ bring hope?
- Tell of a time when you felt hopeless.
- What's the difference between hoping for something and praying for something?

TALK ABOUT...

CONCLUDING PRAYER:

God, give us the strength and the wisdom to turn to you each day for hope. Give us and all the people of the world a sense of hope so we can cease living lives of desperation and anger. Give us the hope that only you can bring and give us the courage to share that hope with the world. May all who meet us know that we are people who live in the hope of Christ. Hear us now as we pray. Amen.

Love

REFLECTION:

No emotion has been written about more than love, and no three words are used in music and movies as easily as "I love you." And, unfortunately, in an age where love and marriage come and go at an alarming rate, "love" has lost much of its meaning. But the love of God for us is another thing. It doesn't shift with the times. It doesn't fade away when we do. It does not bend to the powers of the world. God's love for us never changes, no matter what we do. And that is the kind of love to which God calls us. Perhaps we can never love with the perfection of God, but we are still called to that perfection, to be "compassionate as our Heavenly Father is compassionate."

SUGGESTED READINGS:

Luke 10:30-37
(The good Samaritan)

1 Corinthians 13: 1-13
(The greatest of these is love)

1 John 3:13-24
(The law of love)

Matthew 22:34-40
(The greatest commandment)

Matthew 25:31-46
(Loving others as Christ)

THINK ABOUT....

- What does it mean to love?
- How do you know when someone loves you?
- How does the love we have for each other differ from the love God has for us?
- Write on a piece of paper the names of the people whom you love and the names of those whom you believe love you.
- What does it mean to love your neighbour as yourself?

TALK ABOUT...

CONCLUDING PRAYER:

Lord, teach us to love and help us to be more considerate of those we love. In our families, at work and at school, and even to strangers, we pray that we may be witnesses to the love you have given us all. May others see in us your love shining bright. In everything that we say and do, may your love be seen. Hear us now as we pray. Amen.

Peace & War

REFLECTION:

An unfortunate fact of our world is that somewhere tonight there is a war raging. Bullets are flying. Frightened people hide behind locked doors and hope the next bomb will not fall on their home. Somewhere tonight people are hungry and children lie crying and sleepless on a dusty piece of Earth. And yet, as Christians we know that through all of this God is moving, touching and healing. It is our faith that tells us that there is more than what we can understand and see. Seeking peace in the world can seem a hopeless task. So what are we to do as Christians? We do what we can. We pray. We touch one person at a time and believe that peace is stronger than hatred, that God is stronger than the world.

SUGGESTED READINGS:

Luke 15:11-32
(The prodigal son)

John 20:19-29
(Peace be with you)

Isaiah 41:10-16
(Do not be afraid)

Ephesians 6:10-20
(The spiritual war)

THINK ABOUT...

- Why do you think there is war?
- Is peace more than just "not war"?
- Read the newspaper or watch the television news together and pray for the victims of war.
- Is it ever okay to kill another person?
- Do you believe one person can make a difference in issues of war and peace?
- As Christians, what should we do for the victims of war?

TALK ABOUT...

CONCLUDING PRAYER:

We pray for peace, Lord. We ask for a world of perfection that only you can give. Grant us all a peace that begins in our own hearts and souls and then spreads like a wild fire across plains and mountains, touching one person at a time. Give us peace. Help us to teach peace to those around us. Let the world know you and your peace through us. Hear us now as we pray. Amen.

Answering the Call

REFLECTION:

In John 15, Jesus says these words: "It was not you who chose me, but I who chose you." This is real news for many of us, for it's easy to get this idea in our heads that somehow we "choose" to follow Christ. But no matter what we think, no matter how many choices we make about our faith, the fact remains that we are the ones who have been chosen. We are like children who do not choose our parents but nevertheless choose to love them and accept their guidance and protection. We Christians are not a special bunch because we've chosen our lot in life, but because we have been hand-picked for the service of God. We are not responsible, but we must respond.

THINK ABOUT...

- What does it mean to be called by God?
- How do we hear God's voice in our world?
- What do you think you are called to do in your life right now?
- How does it feel to be chosen to do something?
- Tell about a person you know who you think is responding to a call from God.

TALK ABOUT...

CONCLUDING PRAYER:

Lord, open our ears and our eyes so that we may respond to your call. Help us to remember that it was you who chose us and not we who chose you. Thank you for choosing us to be your people, and for giving us your son, Jesus, to be our saviour and friend. May we respond to your call with the same kind of enthusiasm and commitment shown by the first disciples. Hear us now as we pray. Amen.

Peer Pressure and Making Decisions

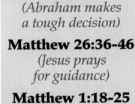

REFLECTION:

Whether you are a child, a teenager or an adult, decisions can be hard to make at times. It's important to acknowledge that "peer pressure" is not something that only affects teenagers. We can all be swayed on occasion by the opinions and lifestyles around us, even when we know we're not making the "right" decision. But as Christians, we have been given the wonderful gift of the Holy Spirit. Do we seek out the help of the Spirit when we need to make decisions? Do we take the time to reflect on important decisions and pray about them, or do we just go with our "gut" feelings? If we remember that the Spirit's help is there for the taking, our next decision might be much easier.

SUGGESTED READINGS:

Romans 7:14-25
(The inner struggle)

Genesis 22:1-19
(Abraham makes a tough decision)

Matthew 26:36-46
(Jesus prays for guidance)

Matthew 1:18-25
(Joseph faces a tough decision)

THINK ABOUT...

- What was the last bad decision you made?
- When was the last time you prayed about a decision?
- Discuss the types of peer pressure you face at work and at school.
- How do you deal with that pressure?
- Draw up a family contract that states that all important decisions regarding the family and the people in it are to be prayed about and discussed.
- Have everyone sign the contract and keep it in a safe place.

TALK ABOUT...

CONCLUDING PRAYER:

Lord, give us the wisdom to seek the guiding hand of the Holy Spirit in our lives. Help us to make good decisions and deliver us from the temptations that cloud our ability to reason. Help our friends and family remember to turn to you in times of crisis and indecision. Fill our hearts with love for you so that we may always seek to do your will. Hear us now as we pray. Amen.

Being Thankful

SUGGESTED READINGS:

1 Chronicles 16:8-36
(Give thanks to the Lord)

Luke 17: 11-19
(One leper returns thankful)

Acts 2:42-47
(The early church celebrates)

Romans 8:31-39
(A hymn of thanksgiving)

Psalm 100
(A psalm of thanksgiving)

REFLECTION:

Our world is filled with beauty and majesty, and because we are so surrounded by this grandeur, we sometimes take it all for granted. The natural wonders of the Earth are so powerful that we imagine that they must have a life of their own. But they do not; they are creations of the Creator and they shout of the handiwork of God. And so we need to be thankful for the world and everything in it that sustains, entertains and inspires us. There is more that moves the ocean to the shore than the tide. There is more that forms the canyons than the rushing river. Throughout our world there is the guiding hand of God, and for that we are thankful.

THINK ABOUT...

- Say the things you are thankful for.
- Create a family prayer book where anyone can write down things for which they are thankful and things and people for whom they want to pray. Read from the book during family prayer times.
- What does it mean when we don't stop and thank God?
- What do you think are God's most marvellous gifts to the world?

TALK ABOUT...

CONCLUDING PRAYER:

Lord, thank you for all you have given us. Forgive us for all the times when we fail to stop and say thank you. We receive so many blessings in so many ways that often we just forget that all our blessings come from you. Thank you for the wonderful gifts you have given the world, all the beauty that you give just for us to enjoy. Hear us now as we pray. Amen.

Discerning and Using Gifts

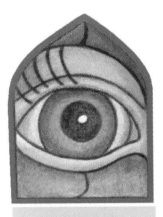

REFLECTION:

Part of our call as Christians is to effectively use the gifts given to us by God. Part of that call includes simply figuring out what our gifts are. So often the label of "gifted" is only attached to people like artists and musicians, and so many people wander about thinking they have no gifts. You may not be a great leader or a creative genius, but you may have a kind heart and a listening ear for a person who just needs someone to listen. You may have loving arms that can rock a sick infant to sleep. Somewhere in each of us there is a God-given gift waiting to be used. As Christians, we are called to uncover that gift and use it for the glory of God.

SUGGESTED READINGS:

Matthew 25:14-30
(Parable of the talents)

Matthew 2:1-12
(Visit of the Magi)

1 Corinthians 12:1-11
(Spiritual gifts)

1 Corinthians 12: 12-31
(We are all one body)

Luke 20:45-21:4
(The widow's mite)

THINK ABOUT...

- What does it mean to be gifted?
- Tell at what you think you are gifted.
- Tell at what you think the others in your family are gifted.
- Who are the people you know who best use their gifts for the glory of God?
- How are you using your gifts for the glory of God?

TALK ABOUT...

CONCLUDING PRAYER:

Lord, help us to see our own giftedness and use our talents to glorify your name. We ask you to take our humble gifts and multiply them so they can work wonders here on Earth, just as once Jesus multiplied a few fish and loaves of bread into a feast for the hungry people. We may not have much to offer, but we give you all we have. Hear us now as we pray. Amen.

Serving and Being Served

REFLECTION:

Saint Basil once asked: "If you live alone, whose feet will you wash?" In this succinct question, Basil points out two important elements of our lives as Christians – service and community. Because the opposite of Basil's question also holds true: "If you live alone, who will wash your feet?" Peter objected to having his feet washed by Jesus, but Jesus set him straight, reminding him and the other disciples that they must be willing to let their Christian brothers and sisters care for them. Sometimes it is easier to give help than it is to receive it because our pride can get in the way. But we must be willing to do both, otherwise we are denying others the opportunity to serve. Jesus was clear about serving: The one who serves is the greatest.

SUGGESTED READINGS:

John 13:1-16
(Jesus washes the disciples' feet)

Luke 10:30-37
(The good Samaritan)

Luke 10:38-42
(Mary and Martha)

Luke 22:24-27
(Who is the greatest?)

Matthew 25:31-46
(Loving others as Christ)

THINK ABOUT...

- Do you like to be served? Why?
- To whom do you offer yourself in service?
- Who serves you?
- Wash each other's feet.
- Line up front to back and do a group back rub. Switch the line around so everyone gets a chance to rub everyone else's back.

TALK ABOUT...

CONCLUDING PRAYER:

Lord God, thank you for giving us Jesus as the ultimate example of what it means to serve. Help us to follow in his example and go to others in need with open hearts and a willingness to offer ourselves in service. Show us how to allow others to help us during our times of need. Thank you for all the people you put in our lives who help us through the tough times. Hear us now as we pray. Amen.

Death

REFLECTION:

Death, although a natural part of life, never ceases to stun us with its brutal finality: We will never see this person again here on earth. No matter what we believe of the after-life, we are still saddened because we will not have this person in our lives. A piece of us has gone. And in our grief we can sometimes wonder if there is anything we can cling to that will always remain. But as Christians we can rejoice in the fact that the Word of God and the promises God makes will never change. The Word of God remains solid, a place of retreat from the changing world. God rides high and bright above the laws of change, presenting a beacon of hope for those who seek the light.

THINK ABOUT…

● Name people who have died and recall something special about their lives. How did the way they lived affect you?
● What's your idea of heaven?
● Are you afraid of dying?
● Visit a cemetery where family members are buried, recall those people, and pray over each grave.
● What's your first memory of someone dying?

TALK ABOUT…

SUGGESTED READINGS:

1 Thessalonians 4:13-18
(Those who have died in Jesus)

1 Corinthians 15:12-34
(Resurrection from the dead)

John 11:1-44
(Lazarus raised from the dead)

John 6:44-51
(I am the bread of life)

Revelation 21:1-8
(A new heaven and a new Earth)

CONCLUDING PRAYER:

Thank you, Lord, for being our solid foundation in an ever-changing world. Thank you for the people you put in our lives who can give us the solace we need in times of despair and remind us that love will be there when all else fades. May your love, shining through them, always pulls us through. Thank you for the gift of life on Earth and the promise of life to come. Hear us now as we pray. Amen.

Life, Birth and Children

REFLECTION:

What our children "become," what they "grow up to be," is one of the basic worries of parenthood. Parents do need to plan for their children's future and help them reach their own goals, but sometimes in all our planning we can forget how wonderful it is to just be a child. For isn't that what God – as a loving parent – wants for us? God has given us two of the greatest gifts imaginable (and they are not so unlike what parents give their children): life itself and the blessing of being called children of God. What we will become is not clear, but there is great comfort simply in being the child of a God who readily and earnestly calls children to "come unto me."

SUGGESTED READINGS:

Mark 10:13-16
(Jesus and the children)

Luke 2:41-50
(Young Jesus in the Temple)

Jeremiah 1:1-10
(Jeremiah was chosen before he was born)

Genesis 21:1-7
(The birth of Isaac)

THINK ABOUT...

● On the birthdays of family members, don't forget to thank God for life.
● Why does Jesus want us all to become like children?
● Why is it important to guard the sanctity of life?
● What is it like to hold a very young baby?
● Babies have to rely on their parents for everything.
● Discuss how our relationship with God is similar.

TALK ABOUT...

CONCLUDING PRAYER:

Lord, thank you for the gift of life. May we never take this gift lightly and may we never forget that all life comes from you. Thank you for the wonderful bodies and minds you give us so we can enjoy life and grow to become your servants. Please protect all the babies, Lord, especially those who are yet to be born. Give them a chance to enjoy your beautiful world. Hear us now as we pray. Amen.

The Eucharist

REFLECTION:

A few days after Jesus' crucifixion, two of his disciples meet him on the road but are unable to recognise him. Such fools, we think. How can they not see? But then Jesus breaks bread with them and their eyes are opened. Here we are, 2,000 years later, and we know we are supposed to recognise Christ in the faces of all those in need. Yet sometimes we just can't seem to see. God knows our weaknesses. He knows that sometimes we need a sign, something to grab onto. So God has given us the Eucharist. And as we accept the broken body and spilled blood of our Lord in our outstretched hands, a miracle occurs: our eyes are opened.

SUGGESTED READINGS:

Luke 24:13-35
(The road to Emmaus)

Matthew 26:26-29
(The last supper)

1 Corinthians 12
(The body of Christ)

Acts 2:42-47
(The early Church shares the Eucharist)

John 6:52-58
(The bread of life)

THINK ABOUT...

- How important is the Eucharist to you?
- What does it do for you?
- Bake unleavened bread together (just flour and water) and discuss the power of being able to share in the body of Christ.
- Tell what you remember about your First Communion.
- How do you prepare yourself to receive communion?
- Do you prepare yourself?

TALK ABOUT...

CONCLUDING PRAYER:

Lord, thank you for providing us with an outward sign of your love for us, for we are sometimes weak and need to remember all you have done for us and given us. Thank you for the gift of your son, Jesus, and for the gift of the Eucharist, which helps us remember his death and his resurrection and our source of salvation. Help us to never receive this precious gift lightly or take it for granted. Hear us now as we pray. Amen.

Dealing with Conflict

REFLECTION:

Conflict, in whatever form it might take (fighting, arguing, unspoken rage, unforgiveness, etc.), is a part of our lives. In many ways we are not healthy without it. Conflict, when dealt with, often clarifies and solidifies relationships. It could even be true that relationships are not strong until they have been tested by the fires of conflict. But there is also a danger in letting conflict have too much control in our lives. Jesus never went out of his way to avoid conflict (remember the money changers in the Temple?) but he is clear that, as his followers, we are to base our lives on love, understanding and compassion and use these virtues to overcome conflict when it enters our lives.

THINK ABOUT...

- How does this family deal with conflict?
- Why is it important to deal with conflicts and not just ignore them?
- What's the worst fight you ever had with another person? Did you ever work it out?
- Discuss any current conflicts between family members and how they can be resolved.
- What's easier for you to do: ask for forgiveness or forgive another person? Why?

TALK ABOUT...

CONCLUDING PRAYER:

Lord, there will always be conflicts in our lives, always times when we choose to argue and fight instead of love. We ask that you help us make those times few. Give us the strength and the courage to put love before pride. And when conflicts do arise, give us the wisdom to resolve them quickly. Help us to readily forgive those around us and seek their forgiveness for ourselves. Hear us now as we pray. Amen.

When Marriage Breaks Down

REFLECTION:

Marriages do break down and it is not always helpful to try to apportion blame. Sometimes it is best for couples to separate. Divorce is becoming increasingly common and many of us will have experienced it among our own relations or we will know someone affected closely by it. The teaching of Christ, and the teaching of the Church, continues to put before us the high ideal of consecration in Marriage for the whole of life. This is to express the meaning of total love for life, the sort of love revealed in Christ's love for the Church. Human weakness sometimes makes the living of the Marriage vows difficult and the need of the strength of God's love is always there.

SUGGESTED READINGS:

1 Corinthians 13:1-13
(Love never fails)

Matthew 19:1-9
(Jesus on divorce)

Genesis 2:18-25
(God gives Adam a wife)

John 2:1-11
(The wedding feast at Cana)

THINK ABOUT...

● Why do you think Jesus and the Church take their stance against divorce?

● Because divorce is so prevalent in the world today, do you worry about your own family?

● Do you think a couple to whom faith is important has a better chance of staying together?

● What do you think couples need to do to remain married?

TALK ABOUT...

CONCLUDING PRAYER:

God, bless married couples who have chosen to serve you through the ministry of family and home life. Give them the strength to remain faithful to each other and to the vows they made before you. Help them to see the value of the work they do in raising children, no matter how unappreciated they may feel at times. Help them be witnesses to the world of your love and grace. Hear us now as we pray. Amen.

Difficult Times

REFLECTION:

When we witness a major disaster on television or know someone who has been through a heart-wrenching tragedy such as the death of a child, we often ask ourselves how we would cope in such a situation. Even if we have a strong faith, we know that even that could be stretched to the breaking point under such circumstances. Having faith in God doesn't mean we won't feel the pain of loss, but there is solace to be found in our belief in God, even in spite of the sting of death. And while we are certainly not called to daily dwell upon death and the imminent dangers of living in the 20th century, as Christians we can earnestly prepare our hearts and souls for whatever the world throws at us.

SUGGESTED READINGS:

Luke 21:34-36
(Be alert)

Mark 5:21-43
(Jairus' daughter raised to life)

Mark 13:5-13
(The beginning of sorrows)

Matthew 27:45-56
(The death of Jesus)

THINK ABOUT...

● Name some sad things you have witnessed either in your life or in the news.
● Can you pray when sad things happen to you?
● What do you say to God?
● Do you think it's better to forget terrible things (like wars and murders) or remember them?
● How can God help us through these tough times?
● How can we support each other during these times?

TALK ABOUT...

CONCLUDING PRAYER:

Lord, keep us safe from the evil in the world, and give us the confidence to always turn to you in times of trial. Give our family two things: the strength to support each other in times of tragedy and loss, and a sense of our own weakness so we know when it's time to fall on our knees and offer our lives and needs to you. Hear us now as we pray. Amen.

Seeking God

REFLECTION:

As Christians, we seek God. We try to find God in our lives. Sometimes we try harder than other times. In the Acts of the Apostles, Paul talks about "seeking" for God. Seek is a strong word. It may entail desperation and passion. You really want something when you seek for it. When loved ones are dying, when relationships are failing, when we fear for the health or the souls of our children, it is during those times that we seek for God and shed tears of desperation and pain. God understands those emotions and hears our pleas, but there is also comfort in knowing that our God also listens when we pray our everyday, half-hearted prayers like: "just get me through this day, Lord."

SUGGESTED READINGS:

Acts 17:23-28
(Seeking for God)

Luke 12:13-21
(Seeking wealth)

Mark 3:7-12
*The crowds
follow Jesus)*

Matthew 6:25-34
(God will provide)

THINK ABOUT...

- What things do you want most in your life?
- What do you seek?
- What do you long for?
- What does it mean to seek God?
- Where do you find God in your life?
- What do you expect of God?
- What do you think God expects of you?

TALK ABOUT...

CONCLUDING PRAYER:

Lord, give us the grace to search for you every day, seeking you out and finding you in the sometimes all-too-infrequent quiet moments of our lives as well as the all-too-common busy and noisy times. Give us the wisdom to know that you hear all our prayers, large or small, important or insignificant. Give us glimpses of your glory, Lord, so we will continue to seek you. Hear us now as we pray. Amen.